I0605730

HORSE BREEDS

APPALOOSA

BY WHITNEY SANDERSON

Kids Core

An Imprint of Abdo Publishing
abdobooks.com

abdobooks.com

Printed in the United States of America, North Mankato, Minnesota.
052025
092025

Cover Photo: Shutterstock Images
Interior Photos: Duncan Moody/iStockphoto, 4–5; Margo Harrison/Shutterstock Images, 6; iStockphoto, 9, 22, 23 (top); Shutterstock Images, 10, 23 (bottom), 26, 29; Fine Art Images/Heritage Images/Hulton Archive/Getty Images, 12–13; Transcendental Graphics/Archive Photos/Getty Images, 15; William Mullins/Alamy, 17; Carl Iwasaki/The Chronicle Collection/Getty Images, 18; Rita Kochmarjova/Shutterstock Images, 20–21; Dorling Kindersley/Universal Images Group/Newscom, 23 (middle); Tom McGinty/Shutterstock Images, 24; Julia Remezova/Shutterstock Images, 28

Editor: Marie Pearson
Series Designer: Ryan Gale

Library of Congress Control Number: 2024949330

Publisher's Cataloging-in-Publication Data

Names: Sanderson, Whitney, author.
Title: Appaloosa / by Whitney Sanderson
Description: Minneapolis, Minnesota: Abdo Publishing, 2026 | Series: Horse breeds | Includes online resources and index.
Identifiers: ISBN 9781098297480 (lib. bdg.) | ISBN 9798384930006 (ebook)
Subjects: LCSH: Appaloosa horse--Juvenile literature. | Horses--Juvenile literature. | Horse breeds--Juvenile literature. | Zoology--Juvenile literature.
Classification: DDC 636.1--dc23

CONTENTS

Appaloosas can make fun show jumping horses.

A COLORFUL PERFORMER

Mia cantered Party in a circle in front of the course of jumps. She noticed people in the audience smiling and even pointing. Party often got a lot of attention, with her white coat covered in dark brown spots.

In show jumping, the horse and rider work together to clear jumps quickly without dropping bars.

But this was show jumping. It was her performance that mattered, not her color.

Mia pointed Party toward a fence with red-and-white striped poles. She felt Party's strides quicken. Three, two, one, liftoff! Then a sharp turn to the second fence, a brick wall. Party sailed over it. Now on to a triple combination. They were really flying now. Too fast, Mia realized. Party needed a shorter, more powerful stride to make it over three jumps in a row.

Mia sat back and put steady pressure on the reins. Party listened to Mia and shifted her weight back. Jump, jump, jump! They made it over all three fences.

Party jumped fast and clean through the rest of the course. Soon they reached the last fence, a water jump. Party didn't like those. Mia felt Party's body curve sideways. She wanted to go around the sparkling pool, not over it. Mia closed her legs around Party's sides to urge her forward. Party took a short, choppy stride, then a big one. She was going for it! They cleared the water jump and galloped past the finish line. A clear round!

Mia gave Party a big pat on the neck and told her, “Great job!” She loosened the reins to let the horse stretch as they cantered in a circle to cool off. Mia was proud. It was Party’s first time show jumping, and she had done her best. Mia was sure that her clever and beautiful Appaloosa would continue to shine in their favorite sport.

Ancient Art

Cave paintings from 20,000 years ago show spotted horses. The paintings show that spotted horses have appeared in wild horse herds for at least that long. But the Appaloosa is the first horse to be bred on purpose for this pattern.

The Appaloosa is the state horse of Idaho.

Spotted Horse

The Appaloosa is a breed of horse best known for its spotted coat. This is a smart, sturdy horse that competes in many riding sports.

An Appaloosa with a small spotted area may be born to a mother with no obvious spots.

Appaloosas are light horses, which means they are mostly used for riding rather than pulling heavy loads.

More than half a million Appaloosa horses have been **registered** in the United States. About 10,000 new horses are registered each year. Appaloosas are well known for their colorful looks and athletic skills.

Further Evidence

Look at the website below. Does it give any new evidence to support Chapter One?

Appaloosa Horses

abdocorelibrary.com/appaloosa

A painting from the 1600s shows a spotted horse.

CHAPTER 2

HISTORY OF THE APPALOOSA

Spanish settlers first brought horses to North America in the 1500s. Some horses escaped and formed wild herds. The Nimiipuu (Nez Perce) people of Idaho, Oregon, and Washington caught some of these wild horses. They started breeding spotted horses.

They used horses for transport and companionship in daily life. They also used the horses to hunt large animals, especially bison.

The Nimiipuu needed horses that were brave, fast, and strong. They especially valued horses with spotted coats. By the mid-1700s, the Appaloosa breed took shape. The Nimiipuu eventually called these horses Maamin. European settlers called them Palouse horses.

Maamin

The name Maamin might have come from the word Mormon. Mormon was a historical term for a person belonging to the Church of Jesus Christ of Latter-Day Saints. Nimiipuu may have traded with Mormons to get some spotted horses.

Horses have long been an important part of Nimiipuu culture.

Many of the horses were in a region near the Palouse River in present-day Washington and Idaho. Later, Palouse became Appaloosa.

Nimiipuu riders wore **regalia**. They also made regalia for their horses to wear. It was often made from deer hide. Feathers, fur, and beads decorated it. Many of the designs told stories about the person or animal who wore the regalia.

In 1877, the US Army and Nimiipuu were at war. The US government had forced the Nimiipuu to live on **reservation** land. Then the government made the reservation even smaller. Many Appaloosa horses were killed in the war. Soldiers bred those still alive with draft horses to use for farm work. By the late 1800s, few Appaloosas were left.

Nimiipuu observe many traditions today, including putting regalia on Appaloosas.

Some people in the 1900s had ranches dedicated to raising Appaloosas.

Saving the Breed

A few Nimiipuu and settlers kept breeding Appaloosas. The breed's numbers rose. Some Appaloosas ended up in Wild West shows and early Western films. This let more people know about the breed.

Later, Appaloosas mixed with other breeds. They were bred with quarter horses, Arabians, and mustangs. So Appaloosas today have a variety of sizes and body types.

In 1938, a horse breeder named Claude Thompson started the Appaloosa Horse Club (ApHC). It works to **preserve** the breed. The ApHC holds Appaloosa horse shows.

Explore Online

Visit the website below. Does it give any new information about horses in Nimiipuu culture that wasn't in Chapter Two?

How Appaloosa Horses Keep Nez Perce Traditions Alive

abdocorelibrary.com/appaloosa

Appaloosas can have mottled skin. This skin is pink with dark speckles.

LIVING WITH THE APPALOOSA

An Appaloosa is easy to spot. This is a medium-sized horse. It is usually 14.2 to 16 hands high. A hand is 4 inches (10 cm). Appaloosas weigh between 950 and 1,250 pounds (430 and 570 kg). They are tough and strong.

Each Appaloosa's pattern is one of a kind.

Each Appaloosa has a base color, such as **chestnut**, **bay**, black, or gray. Appaloosas can have one of several coat patterns. A few are solid colored. Spotted or solid, every Appaloosa must have at least one other feature of the breed. These are mottled skin, striped hooves, or visible sclerae, which are the white parts of the eyes. Some Appaloosas have short, thin manes and tails.

Appaloosa Patterns

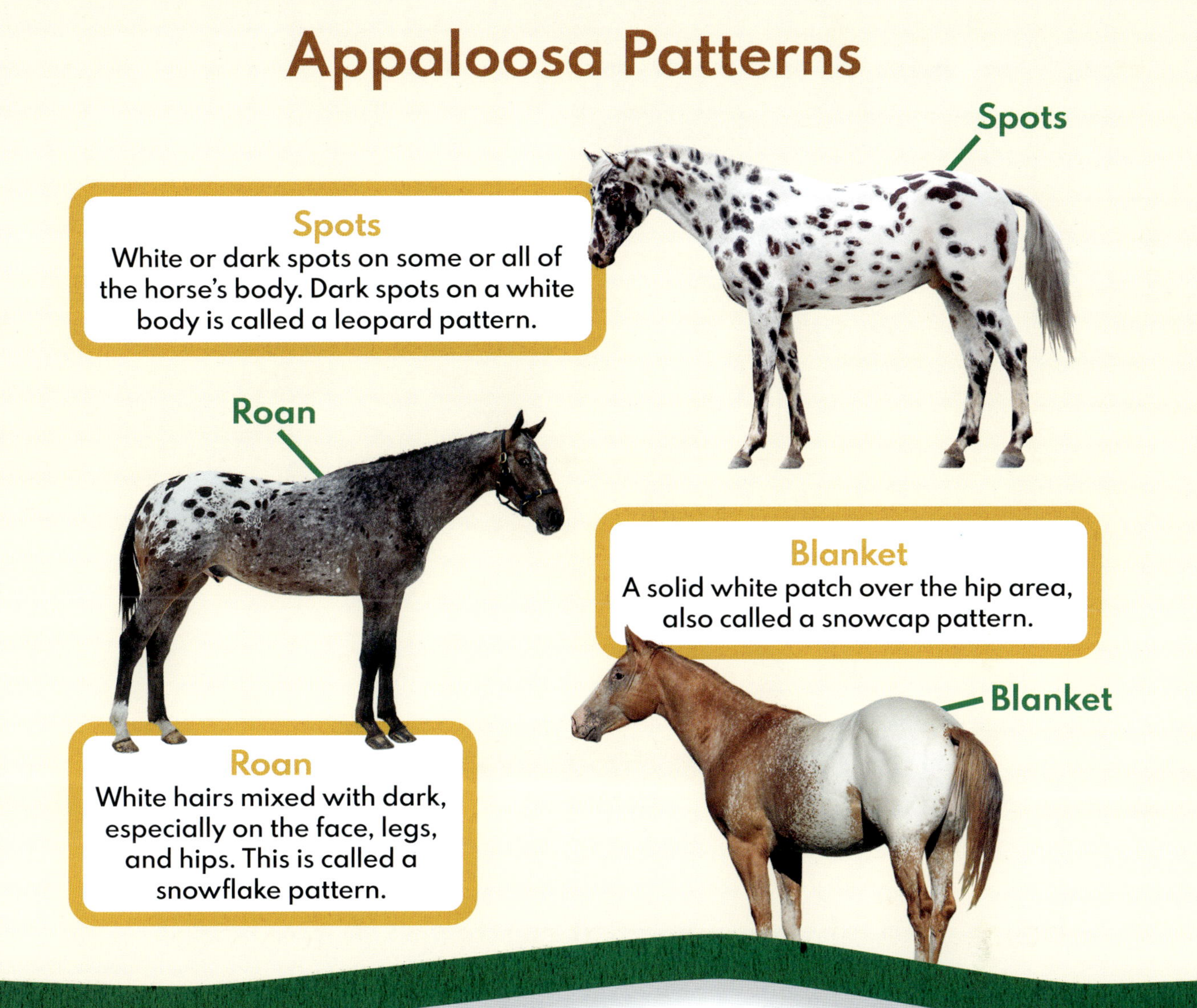

There are three basic coat patterns for an Appaloosa horse. These are blanket, spots, and roan. An Appaloosa can have any mix of these patterns, such as a roan blanket with spots.

Appaloosas are smart, kind, and loyal. The breed can be strong willed. Riders must learn how to **motivate** their horses.

Appaloosas can compete in barrel racing.

A Talented Breed

Appaloosas are common in Western riding sports, such as calf roping and barrel racing. There are also races just for Appaloosas. They usually take place over distances of about half a mile (0.8 km).

People have increasingly chosen Appaloosas for English riding sports, such as jumping and dressage. In dressage, the horse and rider make a pattern of graceful movements at a walk, trot, and canter. The breed used to face challenges in English riding sports. There are many rules about how a horse and rider should look. Solid-colored horses were seen as proper. Appaloosa coloring was seen as too distracting.

Nez Perce Horses

In 1994, Nimiipuu breeders began crossing Appaloosas with the Akhal-Teke, an athletic breed from Central Asia. They created the Nez Perce horse. It is meant to be similar to the original Maamin that once lived alongside the Nimiipuu.

Some people enjoy riding their Appaloosas on land around a barn.

That opinion has been changing. Appaloosas such as Pay N Go have shown they have the skill to match their eye-catching looks. Pay N Go lived from 1984 to 2014. He competed in dressage. Pay N Go was known for his elegant, sweeping strides.

The Appaloosa is a colorful breed. It means a lot to the Nimiipuu people. Many others also appreciate these unique horses.

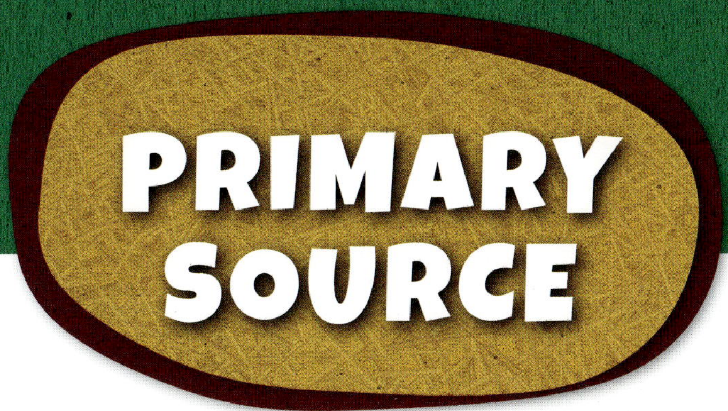

In an online article, Appaloosa owner Evelien Deelen wrote:

> Appaloosas . . . have very distinct personalities, and yet they are accessible for people with all sorts of skill levels. I think that is what I like most about these horses—Appaloosas are suitable for anyone and any purpose.

Source: Evelien Deelen. "Appaloosa Member Spotlight: An International Perspective." *Northwest Horse Source*, 6 May 2021, nwhorsesource.com. Accessed 25 Sept. 2021.

Comparing Texts

Think about the quote. Does it support the information in the chapter? Or does it give a different perspective? Explain how in a few sentences.

BREED TRAITS

White-rimmed eyes
Mottled skin

Glossary

bay
brown with a black mane and tail

chestnut
a solid brown color, ranging from golden to dark brown

motivate
to use a reward that someone wants to encourage them to do something

preserve
to keep something safe

regalia
decorative clothing worn for special occasions

registered
listed as a member of an organization

reservation
land set aside by the government for a certain group of people to use

Online Resources

To learn more about Appaloosas and other horses, visit our free resource websites below.

Visit **abdocorelibrary.com** or scan this QR code for free Common Core resources for teachers and students, including vetted activities, multimedia, and booklinks, for deeper subject comprehension.

Visit **abdobooklinks.com** or scan this QR code for free additional online weblinks for further learning. These links are routinely monitored and updated to provide the most current information available.

Learn More

Bird, F. A. *Nez Perce*. Abdo, 2022.

My Book of Horses and Ponies. DK, 2024.

Ventura, Marne. *Horses*. Abdo, 2023.

Index

About the Author

Whitney Sanderson grew up riding horses as a member of a 4-H club and competing in local horse shows. She is the author of numerous children's books.